Cybersecurity Essentials for SMBs

A Practical Guide to Safeguard Your Business Against Modern Threats

Written by
Eric LeBouthillier

AcraSolution | 2025 1st Edition
www.acrasolution.com

Preface

In today's technology-driven world, cybersecurity is critical. Threats continue to evolve, targeting everything from employee inboxes to cloud infrastructure. This eBook outlines a comprehensive defense strategy across fifteen chapters, each focusing on a core pillar of cybersecurity. It begins with foundational topics like password security, multi-factor authentication, endpoint protection, and zero trust principles. You'll then learn best practices for backups, employee training, secure network setups, and rapid incident response.

Subsequent chapters emphasize ongoing security assessments, managing risks from external vendors, and specialized defenses like email filtering, mobile device management, and data encryption. As remote work becomes more prevalent, VPNs play a vital role in connecting distributed teams securely. Finally, the eBook concludes with a look at cyber insurance, which can help organizations recover financially in the event of a breach. Each chapter is designed to help you bolster your defenses and adapt to an evolving threat landscape, offering actionable guidance for IT professionals, business leaders, and individuals alike.

— ***Eric LeBouthillier***
Author & Cybersecurity Strategist

ISBN: 9798280038448
First Edition

Published by AcraSolution

www.acrasolution.com

LEGAL DISCLAIMER

This eBook is provided for informational purposes only and does not constitute legal, financial, or professional advice. The author and publisher have made every reasonable effort to ensure the accuracy and completeness of the information contained herein; however, neither assumes any responsibility for errors, omissions, or contrary interpretations of the subject matter.

Readers are encouraged to consult with qualified professionals for specific advice tailored to their individual needs. The mention of any products, services, or third-party entities does not imply an endorsement or guarantee of their effectiveness or suitability. Any application of the strategies and recommendations presented is at the reader's discretion and risk.

The author and publisher shall not be liable for any damages (including, without limitation, direct, indirect, incidental, or consequential) caused by the use, misuse, or interpretation of the information herein. All references to regulatory standards, statutes, or compliance requirements are informational and do not replace official legal counsel.

By reading and applying the concepts in this eBook, you acknowledge that you bear sole responsibility for the outcomes of your decisions and actions. If you do not agree to these terms, please discontinue use of this publication immediately.

Table of Contents

CHAPTER 1: STRONG PASSWORD POLICY + MFA

INTRODUCTION

Imagine your passwords as the keys to a digital fortress. If those keys are weak or easily guessable, intruders can walk right in. Strengthening these "keys" is the first and most essential layer of cyber defense. Combine this with multi-factor authentication (MFA), and you raise the security bar even higher.

UNDERSTANDING STRONG PASSWORDS

Passwords should never be simple words or common phrases. Instead, think of them as secret phrases only you would know. The key characteristics of a strong password are:

- Long (ideally 12 characters or more)
- Random (avoid using dictionary words, birthdays, or common references)
- Unique (never reuse passwords across different sites or services)

Weak vs. Strong Passwords

Weak	Strong
123456	5gz%2ov
password	GiraffeBanana3
letmein	pQn7c$z!
qwerty	Colorful$Sky!

WHY LENGTH AND COMPLEXITY MATTER

A password's strength grows exponentially with every character you add. A short, simple password is like a thin lock that's easy to break. A longer, more complex passphrase makes life difficult for attackers, potentially taking years to crack by brute force.

COMMON MISTAKES TO AVOID

- Using personal info (names, birthdays, addresses) that can be found in public records or on social media
- Recycling the same password for multiple accounts
- Writing passwords on sticky notes or storing them in unsecured documents

MULTI-FACTOR AUTHENTICATION (MFA)

MFA requires at least two separate methods to verify a user's identity. Even if someone knows your password, they won't be able to log in without a second factor, such as a code on your phone or a physical security key.

TYPES OF MFA

- SMS or Email Codes (temporary codes sent by text or email)
- Authenticator Apps (one-time codes generated by apps like Google Authenticator or Microsoft Authenticator)

- Physical Tokens (small hardware devices that confirm your identity)
- Biometrics (fingerprint, facial recognition, or other physical traits)

WHY MFA MATTERS

- Defense in Depth: A stolen password alone isn't enough to gain access
- Real-Time Alerts: You get immediate notifications if someone tries to log in from an unrecognized device
- Flexibility: You can choose different verification methods to fit personal or organizational preferences

IMPLEMENTING A STRONG PASSWORD POLICY

KEY STEPS

1. **Set Minimum Requirements**: Enforce a minimum length (12 characters or more) and require a mix of letters, numbers, and symbols
2. **Educate Users**: Explain why strong passwords and MFA are important, offering tips and tools to simplify the process
3. **Use Password Managers**: These tools store and generate passwords securely, reducing password reuse

4. **Enforce MFA**: Make MFA mandatory for critical accounts or wherever possible

COMMON PITFALLS

- **Skipping Training**: Users might not comply if they don't understand the risks or benefits
- **Infrequent Updates**: Failing to periodically review and update password policies can leave weaknesses unaddressed
- **Partial Adoption**: Leaving some accounts without MFA undermines the entire security effort

CONCLUSION

Strong passwords form the first line of defense, and MFA adds a crucial second barrier. By implementing these measures together, you significantly reduce the risk of unauthorized access. While it might add a small step during each login, the security gains are well worth it. This is one of the most straightforward yet powerful changes you can make to protect personal and organizational data.

NEXT STEPS

These foundational techniques are only the beginning. In the upcoming chapters, we'll explore additional layers of defense—ranging from endpoint protection and backup strategies to cloud access control and beyond. Combining multiple protective measures is the best way to stay resilient in an ever-shifting threat landscape.

CHAPTER 2: ENDPOINT PROTECTION (EDR/ANTIVIRUS)

INTRODUCTION

Endpoints—such as laptops, desktops, and mobile devices—are frequent targets for cybercriminals. A single vulnerable endpoint can become a gateway for attackers to infiltrate an entire network. By deploying reliable Endpoint Detection and Response (EDR) solutions alongside traditional antivirus software, organizations and individuals can fortify their defenses against both known and emerging threats.

WHY ENDPOINT SECURITY MATTERS

The Human Factor: Users may unknowingly download malicious files or click harmful links

Malware Propagation: Infected devices can spread threats across a network if not isolated

Data Sensitivity: Endpoints often hold valuable or confidential information

UNDERSTANDING EDR VS. ANTIVIRUS

Traditional antivirus programs focus on detecting known threats using signature-based methods. EDR goes a step further, employing continuous monitoring and behavioral analysis to spot suspicious activities that might indicate zero-day threats or advanced persistent attacks.

KEY FUNCTIONS OF EDR

Real-time Monitoring: Constantly checks processes, files, and network connections

Behavioral Analysis: Detects anomalies rather than relying solely on known malware signatures

Incident Response Tools: Allows rapid isolation of compromised devices and thorough investigations

Threat Intelligence Integration: Receives ongoing updates to adapt to the latest cyber threats

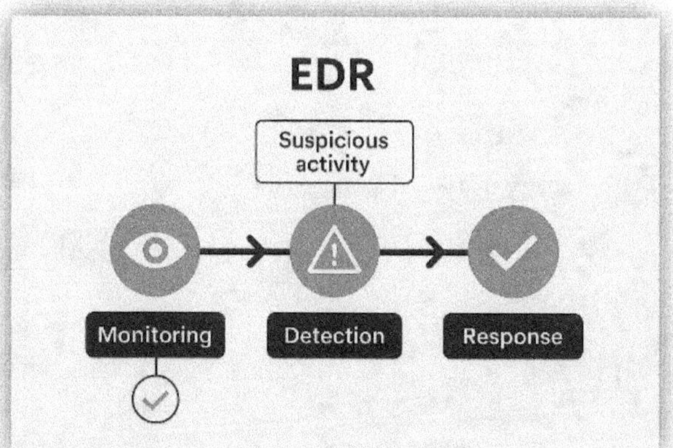

FEATURES TO LOOK FOR IN ENDPOINT SECURITY

- **Automated Updates**: Ensures current threat definitions and security patches
- **Centralized Management**: Simplifies overseeing multiple endpoints and security policies
- **Low Resource Usage**: Prevents software from slowing down user devices
- **Offline Protection**: Guards endpoints even without an active internet connection

BEST PRACTICES

- ✓ **Regularly Patch and Update**: Keep operating systems and apps current to close known vulnerabilities
- ✓ **Conduct Routine Scans**: Schedule automatic scans to catch threats that slip past initial defenses
- ✓ **Combine Signature and Behavior-based Detection**: Leverage both antivirus and EDR capabilities
- ✓ **Train Users**: Employees or family members should know how to spot suspicious links, emails, or apps

COMMON PITFALLS

- **Ignoring Mobile Devices**: Smartphones and tablets often remain unprotected despite storing sensitive information
- **Delaying Updates**: Outdated systems are prime targets for exploitation
- **Overlooking Alerts**: Alerts from security software should be investigated promptly
- **Inconsistent Policies**: Varying requirements across departments or households can leave gaps in protection

CONCLUSION

Securing endpoints is crucial for building a resilient cybersecurity posture. Antivirus software handles known threats, while EDR brings an additional layer of behavioral monitoring and quick response capabilities. By combining technical solutions with user awareness and consistent policy enforcement, you dramatically reduce the risk of data breaches and other malicious activity.

NEXT STEPS

Now that your endpoints are reinforced, it's time to look at other key protective measures—from managing backups to controlling cloud access. Adopting multiple layers of defense helps ensure that even if one barrier fails, others are in place to keep your data and systems safe.

CHAPTER 3: CLOUD ACCESS CONTROL (ZERO TRUST)

INTRODUCTION

The rapid shift to cloud-based services has blurred the traditional network perimeter. In the past, organizations placed great faith in a secure perimeter, assuming that anything inside it could be trusted. Zero Trust turns that assumption upside down, requiring verification and validation at every step—no user or device is automatically trusted. This approach significantly reduces the risk of unauthorized access or data breaches in the cloud.

WHAT IS ZERO TRUST?

Zero Trust is a security framework that treats every access request as potentially hostile. Instead of assuming that all internal users are safe, it continuously verifies identities, devices, and context before allowing access to applications or data. This method is particularly vital for cloud environments, where resources may reside in multiple platforms and locations.

SHIFT FROM TRADITIONAL PERIMETER SECURITY

- **The Old Model**: Establish a strong perimeter (firewall) and trust everything within it
- **The New Model**: Validate each request, regardless of where it originates

KEY PRINCIPLES OF ZERO TRUST

- **Never Trust, Always Verify**: Every user, device, and application must prove its legitimacy
- **Least Privilege Access**: Grant only the minimal level of permissions required to perform a task
- **Micro-Segmentation**: Break the network into smaller zones to isolate resources and minimize damage from breaches
- **Continuous Monitoring and Validation**: Keep an eye on user behavior and device posture at all times

IMPLEMENTING ZERO TRUST FOR CLOUD ACCESS

IDENTITY & ACCESS MANAGEMENT (IAM)

- **Strong Authentication**: Require MFA for all login attempts
- **Role-Based Access Control (RBAC)**: Assign permissions based on specific job roles rather than individuals
- **Automated Provisioning/Deprovisioning**: Quickly grant or remove access when employees join, leave, or change positions

SOFTWARE-DEFINED PERIMETER (SDP)

- **Encrypted Connections**: Enforce secure tunnels for all communications, concealing internal IP addresses
- **Application-Level Access**: Validate each request at the application layer, rather than granting broad network permissions
- **Granular Controls**: Fine-tune who can see what resources, minimizing lateral movement

ACTIVITY MONITORING & ANALYTICS

- **Continuous Logging**: Capture all login attempts, file access, and system changes
- **Anomaly Detection**: Identify and flag unusual behaviors, such as sudden spikes in data transfers
- **Incident Response**: Quickly isolate suspicious devices or user sessions to prevent further damage

BEST PRACTICES

✓ **Integrate Zero Trust Into Existing Security Tools**: Combine it with endpoint protection, firewalls, and intrusion detection systems

✓ **Develop Clear Access Policies**: Ensure all users understand the authentication requirements and acceptable usage policies

✓ **Regularly Review Access Rights**: Conduct periodic audits to confirm that employees still need the privileges they have

✓ **Encrypt Data at Rest and in Transit**: Safeguard sensitive information wherever it resides

COMMON PITFALLS

- **Overly Complex Implementations**: A Zero Trust rollout can become unwieldy if not carefully planned
- **Lack of End-User Education**: Employees may find the additional authentication steps frustrating without proper context
- **Ignoring Shadow IT**: Unapproved applications or cloud services undermine the Zero Trust model's effectiveness
- **Delayed Reactions to Alerts**: Prompt action is essential; ignoring warnings can allow threats to spread

CONCLUSION

Adopting a Zero Trust approach in cloud environments makes unauthorized access significantly harder. By validating every user, device, and request, organizations can maintain tighter control over distributed workloads and data. While it requires thoughtful planning and user buy-in, the payoff is a far more secure cloud ecosystem.

NEXT STEPS

With a Zero Trust model in place for cloud access, your security posture is stronger. However, a comprehensive defense also relies on regular backups, cybersecurity training, and more. In the upcoming chapters, we'll look at additional ways to fortify your systems, from maintaining reliable data backups to developing a robust incident response plan.

CHAPTER 4: DATA BACKUPS (3-2-1 RULE)

INTRODUCTION

Data is at the heart of every organization and individual's digital life—whether it's customer information, financial records, or priceless family photos. Losing this data can be catastrophic, whether the cause is a cyberattack, hardware failure, or simple human error. Implementing a robust backup strategy, such as the 3-2-1 rule, ensures that critical information remains safe and recoverable.

WHAT IS THE 3-2-1 RULE?

The 3-2-1 rule is a straightforward guideline for data protection:

- ✓ **3 Copies of Your Data**: Maintain at least three copies, including the original
- ✓ **2 Different Media**: Store those copies on at least two different types of media (for example, an external hard drive and cloud storage)
- ✓ **1 Offsite Copy**: Keep one backup offsite or in the cloud to protect against localized disasters

WHY BACKUPS ARE ESSENTIAL

RANSOMWARE PROTECTION

A well-structured backup system can save you from paying costly ransoms. If ransomware encrypts your files, you can restore from a clean backup rather than bow to cybercriminals' demands.

HARDWARE FAILURES

Hard drives can fail without warning. Having a backup plan allows quick recovery with minimal downtime.

HUMAN ERROR

Accidental file deletions or overwriting data can happen to anyone. Regular backups ensure mistakes don't become permanent losses.

TYPES OF BACKUP SOLUTIONS

LOCAL BACKUP

Storing data on an external hard drive or network-attached storage (NAS). Although convenient, local backups remain vulnerable to disasters like fires or floods if kept on the same premises.

REMOTE/OFFSITE BACKUP

Sending data to another physical location, such as a secure data center. This offsite approach protects against localized disasters.

CLOUD BACKUP

Utilizing cloud services to store backups. This option offers scalability and easy access, though it requires a stable internet connection and careful attention to security settings.

IMPLEMENTING THE 3-2-1 RULE

1. **Identify Critical Data**: Determine what needs to be backed up—documents, databases, system images, etc.
2. **Schedule Regular Backups**: Automate backups daily, weekly, or monthly, depending on data sensitivity and volume.
3. **Use Multiple Media**: Combine external hard drives, NAS devices, or tape backups for local storage, plus offsite or cloud solutions.

4. **Test Restoration Processes**: A backup is only as good as your ability to restore it. Regularly test data recovery procedures.

BEST PRACTICES

- **Encrypt Backup Data**: Protect sensitive information stored offsite or in the cloud.
- **Versioning**: Keep multiple snapshots of files, ensuring you can roll back to an older copy if needed.
- **Label and Organize**: Clearly identify backups to prevent confusion during an emergency.
- **Monitor Backup Logs**: Ensure every scheduled backup completes successfully and address failures promptly.

COMMON PITFALLS

- **Relying on a Single Backup**: Storing only one backup, especially onsite, puts data at high risk.
- **Infrequent Backups**: Long gaps between backups mean more data could be lost if disaster strikes.
- **Not Testing Restorations**: Many organizations discover backup corruption only when they attempt to restore.
- **Neglecting Secure Storage**: Failing to protect backup media or cloud accounts could expose sensitive data.

CONCLUSION

A proactive backup strategy serves as a safety net against a wide range of disasters. By following the 3-2-1 rule, you increase the odds that your data remains accessible and intact—even in worst-case scenarios. This approach is cost-effective, relatively simple to implement, and often the difference between a minor inconvenience and a business-crippling event.

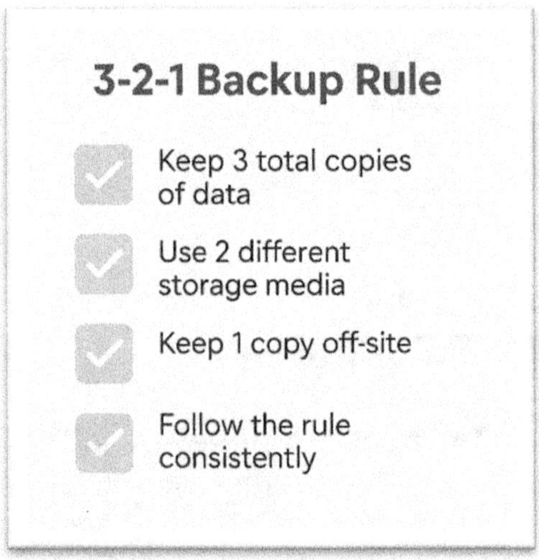

NEXT STEPS

With backups in place, the next focus is on educating the human element of your security environment. A knowledgeable workforce can detect threats early and avoid risky online behavior. Chapter 5 will explore how to foster robust employee cybersecurity awareness, further strengthening your overall defense strategy.

CHAPTER 5: EMPLOYEE CYBERSECURITY AWARENESS TRAINING

INTRODUCTION

Technology can only do so much. Even the most advanced security systems can be undermined by a single uninformed click. Employees, family members, or anyone with access to your digital environment all play a critical role in defense. Cybersecurity awareness training empowers users to recognize and avoid threats before they can do harm.

WHY TRAINING MATTERS

- **Human Error**: Many breaches begin with a well-meaning individual clicking a malicious link or revealing credentials.
- **Social Engineering**: Attackers use manipulation tactics, like phishing or pretexting, to trick people into sharing sensitive information.
- **Compliance Requirements**: Certain industries must prove that employees receive regular security training to meet regulatory standards.

KEY AREAS TO COVER

PHISHING AWARENESS

- **Spotting Red Flags**: Suspicious sender addresses, spelling errors, or urgent calls to action
- **Hovering Over Links**: Verifying the URL before clicking
- **Reporting Procedures**: Employees should know whom to contact if they suspect a phishing attempt

PASSWORD HYGIENE

- **Strong and Unique Passwords**: Emphasize the importance of avoiding reuse
- **Multi-Factor Authentication (MFA)**: Encourage enabling MFA wherever possible
- **Secure Storage**: Discourage writing passwords on sticky notes or saving them in unsecured files

SAFE BROWSING & DEVICE USE

- **Public Wi-Fi Risks**: Understanding the dangers of unencrypted connections
- **Avoiding Malicious Downloads**: Verifying software sources before installation
- **Locking Devices**: Encouraging password-protected screensavers and timeouts

TRAINING METHODS

REGULAR WORKSHOPS OR WEBINARS

- **Interactive Sessions**: Quizzes, breakout discussions, and demonstrations
- **Real-Life Examples**: Share news stories of recent breaches to illustrate the consequences of negligence

SIMULATED PHISHING EXERCISES

- **Hands-On Practice**: Sending test phishing emails to employees helps them identify warning signs
- **Immediate Feedback**: Use the results to tailor further training for those who fall for the simulation

E-LEARNING MODULES

- **Self-Paced Learning**: Allows individuals to complete training at their convenience
- **Tracking Progress**: Administrators can see who has finished modules and who needs a reminder

BEST PRACTICES

1. **Make It Ongoing**: A one-time training session isn't enough. Threats evolve, and so should your curriculum.
2. **Customize Content**: Tailor lessons to your specific industry or organizational culture for maximum relevance.
3. **Foster a No-Blame Culture**: Encourage reporting of mistakes without fear, so that potential breaches can be addressed quickly.
4. **Reward Good Behavior**: Positive reinforcement—like recognition or small incentives—encourages adherence to good practices.

COMMON PITFALLS

- **Overloading with Jargon**: Keep training accessible by avoiding overly technical language.
- **Inconsistent Frequency**: Sporadic or random sessions reduce the likelihood that lessons will stick.
- **Not Measuring Results**: Without tracking who completed training or how they performed, improvements are hard to gauge.
- **Ignoring Management Buy-In**: If leadership doesn't prioritize training, employees may not either.

CONCLUSION

Employee cybersecurity awareness training is the linchpin that unifies all other protective measures. People who can spot suspicious emails, maintain strong passwords, and practice safe browsing significantly lower an organization's overall risk profile. This approach not only protects company data but also encourages a security-first mindset across every level of the organization.

NEXT STEPS

Once your team understands the importance of vigilant online behavior, the next step is to reinforce the technological perimeters of your network. In Chapter 6, we'll explore how proper firewall configurations and secure Wi-Fi setups can further safeguard your environment from external threats.

CHAPTER 6: FIREWALL + SECURE WI-FI CONFIGURATION

INTRODUCTION

Network security starts with a well-configured firewall and a secure Wi-Fi environment. Firewalls act as gatekeepers, filtering incoming and outgoing traffic based on predefined rules. Meanwhile, secure wireless networks help prevent unauthorized access and eavesdropping. Together, they form the first line of defense for both home and corporate networks.

WHY FIREWALLS MATTER

- **Traffic Control**: Firewalls monitor and manage all data entering or leaving the network.
- **Threat Mitigation**: Blocking known malicious IPs, ports, or protocols prevents many common attacks.
- **Regulatory Compliance**: Some industries require evidence of firewall use to meet security standards.

TYPES OF FIREWALLS

NETWORK FIREWALLS

These operate at the perimeter of your network, protecting all devices behind them. Typically found in routers or dedicated hardware appliances, they examine packet headers to decide whether to allow or block traffic.

HOST-BASED FIREWALLS

Installed directly on individual devices, host-based firewalls can customize protection based on the needs of each system. They add an extra layer of defense, especially useful for laptops and mobile devices often used outside a secure corporate environment.

SECURE WI-FI CONFIGURATION

CHOOSING THE RIGHT ENCRYPTION

- **WPA2 or WPA3**: Older standards like WEP are easily breached. WPA2 remains common, but WPA3 offers stronger encryption and improved security.
- **Disable WPS**: Wi-Fi Protected Setup can be exploited if left enabled.

SECURING THE ROUTER OR ACCESS POINT

- **Change Default Credentials**: Avoid leaving the router username and password at factory settings.
- **Use a Strong Wi-Fi Password**: Opt for a long passphrase that's hard to guess.
- **Enable Guest Networks**: Isolate visitors from your main network to limit potential damage if their device is compromised.
- **Keep Firmware Updated**: Regular updates patch vulnerabilities that attackers might exploit.

BEST PRACTICES

1. **Segment Networks**: Separate guest Wi-Fi, IoT devices, and corporate systems to contain breaches.
2. **Implement Intrusion Detection/Prevention Systems (IDS/IPS)**: Additional tools that monitor network traffic for suspicious patterns.

3. **Enable Logging and Alerts**: Monitor firewall logs to spot unusual traffic spikes or repeated access attempts.
4. **Conduct Periodic Security Audits**: Regularly review firewall rules and wireless settings to address evolving threats.

COMMON PITFALLS

- **Overly Permissive Rules**: Opening all ports or allowing unchecked traffic defeats the firewall's purpose.
- **Not Updating Firmware**: Outdated router or firewall software leaves known vulnerabilities unpatched.
- **Insecure Remote Management**: Remote access to your router or firewall should be secured (if needed at all).
- **Ignoring Segmentation**: Mixing sensitive devices with everything else on the same network allows threats to spread easily.

CONCLUSION

A properly configured firewall and secure Wi-Fi setup are foundational elements of any cybersecurity strategy. They help prevent unauthorized access, control data flow, and protect against a range of threats. Whether you manage a corporate network or just want to safeguard your home devices, investing time in strong firewall rules and secure wireless settings pays off in peace of mind.

NEXT STEPS

With a fortified perimeter and secure wireless environment, the next step is to stay current with software and operating system updates. In Chapter 7, we will delve into the importance of patch management, which ensures that known vulnerabilities are quickly addressed before they can be exploited.

CHAPTER 7: SOFTWARE & OS UPDATES (PATCH MANAGEMENT)

INTRODUCTION

Software and operating system updates are often the unsung heroes of cybersecurity. While firewalls and secure Wi-Fi configurations help establish a solid perimeter, patches seal the cracks that attackers target once they're inside—or even before they break in. Patches typically address known vulnerabilities, performance issues, and sometimes introduce new features. As soon as these updates become public, cybercriminals move quickly to exploit any system that remains unpatched. Delaying or ignoring software updates can leave networks, devices, and data dangerously exposed.

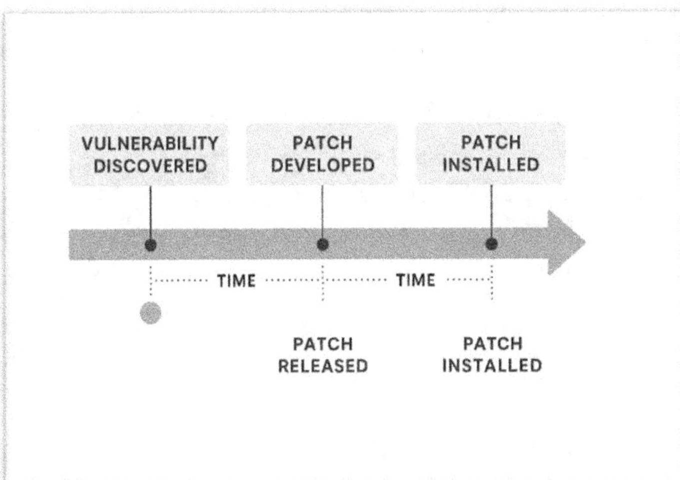

WHY PATCH MANAGEMENT MATTERS

- **Rapidly Evolving Threats**: Attackers monitor patch releases as closely as defenders, using new information to target unpatched systems.
- **Compliance Requirements**: Many regulations, such as HIPAA or PCI DSS, mandate regular updates to address known vulnerabilities.
- **Operational Stability**: Patches often improve performance and fix bugs, reducing the likelihood of crashes or conflicts.

PRIORITIZING UPDATES

Not all patches carry the same weight. Some address minor software bugs, while others close critical security gaps that may already be exploited "in the wild." To deploy patches effectively, focus on those rated as high severity or critical first, ensuring your most vulnerable points are fortified.

This typically involves monitoring vendor announcements, security advisories, and credible news sources. By classifying and applying patches in order of importance, you minimize the time attackers have to exploit serious flaws.

AUTOMATION AND TESTING

Automation

Relying on manual updates can be tedious and error-prone, especially for organizations with numerous devices and applications. Many operating systems and major software suites support automated update processes that run quietly in the background.

Automation speeds deployment, reducing the window in which attackers can capitalize on newly publicized vulnerabilities. However, it's still important to verify successful installation, as some patches may fail silently due to conflicts or other issues.

Testing

Before rolling patches out to critical systems, it's prudent to test them in a controlled environment or on devices that aren't mission-critical. This approach helps identify any incompatibilities or performance issues without jeopardizing your entire network.

Once testing confirms that a patch is stable and effective, a broader deployment can proceed with minimal risk. Logs and monitoring tools play a vital role here, providing alerts if an update fails to install correctly or causes unexpected disruptions.

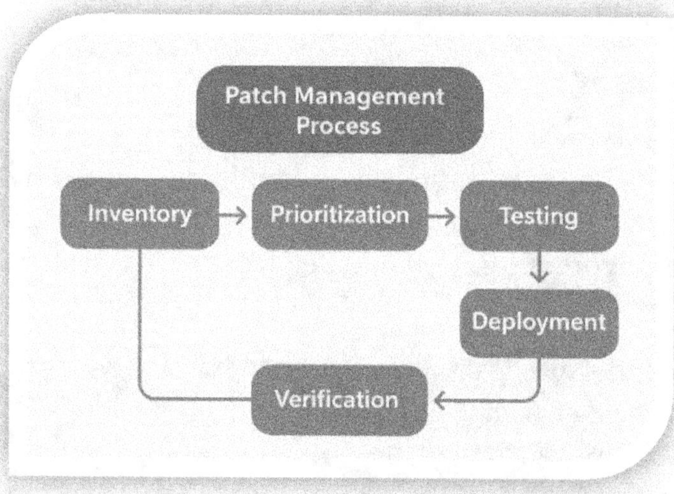

BEST PRACTICES

1. **Maintain an Accurate Inventory**: Keep a detailed list of all hardware, operating systems, and applications to ensure nothing is missed.
2. **Schedule Routine Patching**: Establish regular maintenance windows—like once a month—to encourage consistency and predictability.
3. **Communicate Changes**: Notify users about planned updates, reboot requirements, or downtime to minimize disruption and frustration.

COMMON PITFALLS

- **Ignoring Firmware Updates**: Devices like routers, printers, and IoT equipment can be overlooked, creating hidden entry points for attackers.
- **Partial Coverage**: Updating the operating system but neglecting third-party applications or plugins leaves security gaps.
- **Overlooking Failed Installs**: Automatic updates can fail for specific devices without obvious notifications, requiring regular checks or logs to catch problems.

CONCLUSION

Patch management is a continuous process rather than a one-time task. Every new vulnerability discovered is another reason to review and update your systems. By prioritizing, automating, and carefully testing patches, you can close security gaps that criminals frequently exploit.

NEXT STEPS

Even with thorough patching, no system is impervious to sophisticated attacks or unexpected vulnerabilities. That's why a well-defined plan for handling security incidents is crucial. In Chapter 8: Basic Incident Response Plan, we'll explore how to detect intrusions, contain threats, and recover quickly, ensuring your organization remains resilient in the face of adversity.

CHAPTER 8: BASIC INCIDENT RESPONSE PLAN

INTRODUCTION

Even with strong firewalls, secure Wi-Fi, and diligent patch management, security incidents remain a possibility. Cybercriminals adapt quickly, and no system is entirely foolproof. A Basic Incident Response Plan outlines how to detect threats swiftly, limit damage, and recover without unnecessary chaos. Rather than improvising under pressure, you'll have a clear roadmap for containing breaches, preserving data, and maintaining stakeholder trust.

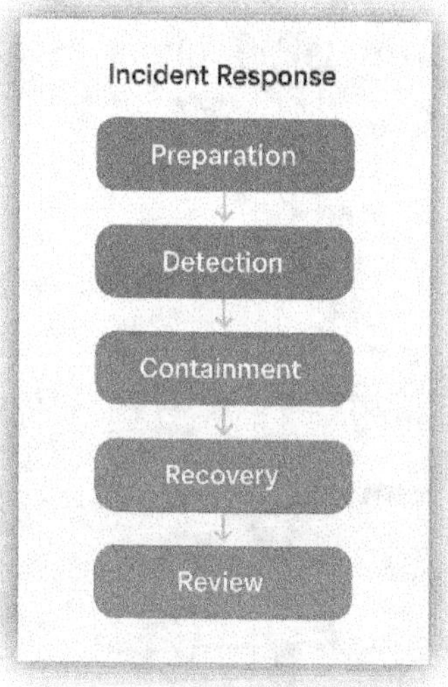

An effective plan extends beyond technical measures. It requires organized teamwork, proper documentation, and thorough communication. By the time a breach makes headlines, security teams are often well into containment efforts.

If you have a structured plan, you can respond decisively, reducing operational downtime and the risk of long-term harm.

WHY INCIDENT RESPONSE MATTERS

• **Rapid Containment**: Quick reactions can keep an intrusion from spreading, saving crucial time and resources.

• **Regulatory Requirements**: Many industries demand proof of proactive security measures, including an established incident response process.

• **Preserving Reputation**: An uncoordinated reaction can deepen mistrust among customers, partners, and the public.

Data breaches that linger undetected allow criminals to exfiltrate information or cause extended harm. By prioritizing incident response, you ensure suspicious activity is spotted sooner, letting you neutralize threats before they escalate.

Strong, documented procedures also demonstrate a firm commitment to security, reassuring both regulators and clients. Ultimately, incidents become opportunities to learn, refine defenses, and foster a more resilient organization.

KEY ELEMENTS OF AN INCIDENT RESPONSE PLAN

• **Roles and Responsibilities**: Assign clear duties. Who investigates alerts? Who handles external notifications? Clarity prevents confusion and delays.

• **Communication Strategy**: Decide how and when to involve management, legal counsel, law enforcement, and customers. Use secure channels to avoid tipping off attackers.

• **Escalation Criteria**: Define thresholds that turn a minor issue into a full-scale incident. Quick escalation ensures key decision-makers are on hand.

• **Documentation**: Meticulous records help you trace the breach's origin, understand how it spread, and refine policies. They're also vital for regulatory or legal inquiries.

A well-crafted plan remains dynamic. Regular reviews keep it aligned with technological changes and shifting business priorities. New software deployments, acquisitions, or staff changes should prompt updates to the plan, ensuring no gaps exist in roles or coverage.

PHASES OF INCIDENT RESPONSE

PREPARATION

This is the backbone of any plan. Invest in training, run simulated drills, and confirm that the right tools—like forensic software or network monitors—are ready. The more prepared you are, the smoother later phases will unfold.

DETECTION & ANALYSIS

Potential incidents often arise from unusual logs, user reports, or automated security alerts. Swift identification hinges on effective monitoring. Once you suspect an incident, analyze logs, examine affected systems, and classify the threat level. Misjudging an event can lead to an overreaction or, worse, an underreaction that leaves attackers free to operate.

CONTAINMENT & ERADICATION

Containment strategies may involve isolating compromised devices or disconnecting specific network segments. The goal is to halt any further spread. Eradication follows, removing malware, disabling infiltrator accounts, or patching exploited vulnerabilities. Both steps demand careful coordination to avoid disrupting legitimate operations or unintentionally destroying critical evidence.

RECOVERY & POST-INCIDENT REVIEW

After neutralizing threats, restore systems from clean backups, ensure vulnerabilities are addressed, and monitor for recurring attacks. A thorough review documents each stage: what happened, how you responded, and what can be improved. This feedback loop updates policies and fosters a stronger defense.

BEST PRACTICES

Keep the plan accessible. It should be concise enough for teams to consult quickly during a crisis. Practice with tabletop exercises or penetration tests to validate assumptions. For each incident, gather as many details as possible—such as user actions and system logs—to paint a complete picture. If feasible, maintain offline copies of critical documents and backups in case attackers target your network tools. And don't overlook mental readiness: even the best plan fails if stress or indecision paralyzes the team.

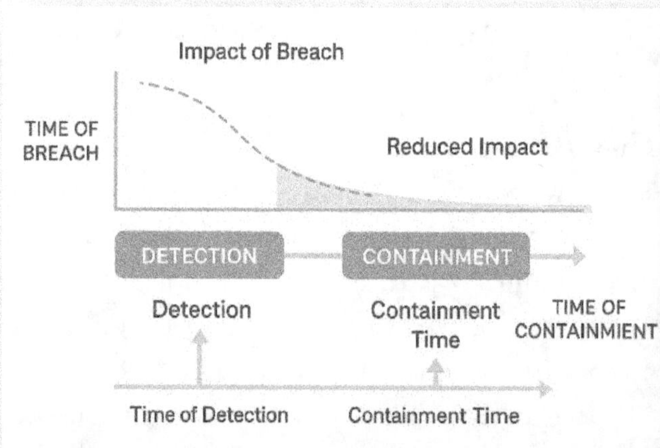

COMMON PITFALLS

• **Underestimating "Minor" Alerts**: Dismissing small anomalies can miss the early stages of a serious breach.

• **Poor Coordination**: Confusion over who's in charge slows containment, giving attackers more time inside the system.

• **Skipping the Review**: Forgoing a post-incident analysis allows repeated mistakes, undermining the plan's long-term benefits.

Another frequent misstep is not testing the plan until a real emergency strikes. Unpracticed teams may panic, overlook vital steps, or duplicate efforts.

Additionally, failing to revise procedures after organizational changes can leave newly acquired systems or software unprotected. Roles may also shift over time, so it's essential to keep everyone's responsibilities current.

CONCLUSION

A Basic Incident Response Plan equips you to handle breaches methodically, limiting the chaos that often accompanies a cyberattack.

Each phase—from preparation and detection to containment and recovery—builds on the last, forming a cohesive cycle of vigilance and continuous learning. Far from being a static document, this plan should evolve in tandem with technological advances and the changing threat landscape.

When an incident does arise, the clarity of preassigned roles, communication pathways, and escalation procedures can be the difference between a contained event and a full-blown disaster.

By adopting this systematic approach, you minimize both immediate losses and long-term fallout, preserving trust among your customers, partners, and workforce. Even if an attack catches you off guard initially, a well-practiced response plan ensures a coordinated, swift effort to restore operations.

Such resilience becomes a competitive advantage, demonstrating to stakeholders and regulators alike that you're committed to protecting valuable data and maintaining business continuity.

NEXT STEPS

To further reduce risk, it's crucial to examine potential vulnerabilities beyond your immediate network. In Chapter 9: Vendor & SaaS Risk Review, we'll explore how to assess and manage risks introduced by third-party providers. With external services often playing critical roles in day-to-day operations, understanding and mitigating these partner risks is an essential part of any comprehensive cybersecurity program.

CHAPTER 9: VENDOR & SAAS RISK REVIEW

INTRODUCTION

Vendors and Software-as-a-Service (SaaS) providers are integral to modern business operations, offering specialized capabilities that support everything from data storage to payment processing. However, each partnership also brings potential security concerns. If a vendor's systems are compromised, attackers may gain access to your own network or sensitive information. As reliance on third-party solutions grows, it's essential to perform regular risk reviews to safeguard your organization.

WHY THIRD-PARTY RISK MATTERS

Cybercriminals view third parties as indirect gateways to larger targets. A single overlooked gap in a vendor's infrastructure can undermine your defenses. Moreover, regulatory standards like GDPR or HIPAA increasingly hold businesses responsible for the security practices of their providers. Demonstrating that you've exercised due diligence in assessing vendor security not only prevents fines and legal trouble but also preserves customer trust.

Conducting a thorough review of a vendor's security posture goes beyond a basic questionnaire. It may include evidence of recognized certifications—such as ISO 27001 or SOC 2—and deeper inquiries about data encryption, retention policies, and incident response procedures. By understanding how vendors manage risk, you can integrate their services with confidence or, if necessary, seek alternatives that better align with your security requirements.

IDENTIFYING & CATEGORIZING VENDORS

Create an inventory of every third party involved in your operations. Sort them by the sensitivity of the data they handle and the potential impact if they're breached.

- **Tier 1**: Access to confidential data or mission-critical services
- **Tier 2**: Handles important but less sensitive information
- **Tier 3**: Performs minor tasks with minimal data exposure

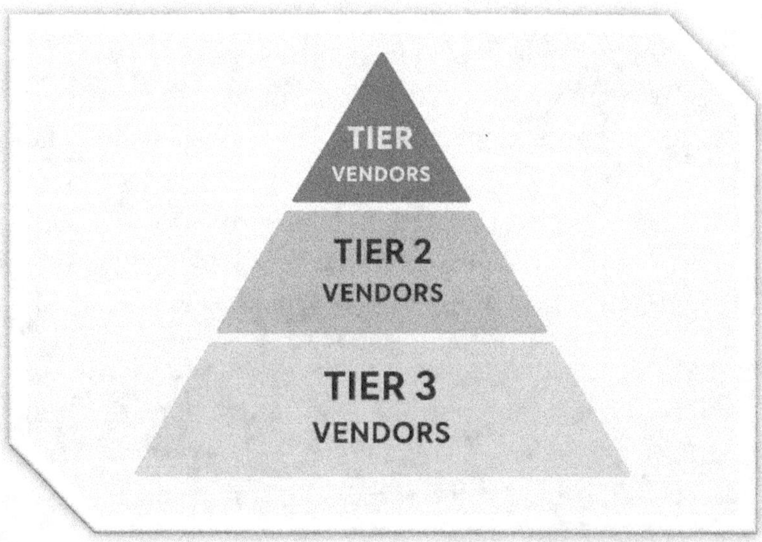

Focusing your most rigorous checks on Tier 1 providers ensures resources are allocated where risk is highest. While Tier 2 and Tier 3 vendors also need assessments, their reviews can be lighter unless there's a reason to suspect increased vulnerability.

DUE DILIGENCE & ASSESSMENTS

Gathering information about a vendor's security may include reviewing documented policies, audit reports, or performing hands-on evaluations. Higher-risk vendors should supply proof of robust security practices, like PCI DSS compliance if they handle payment data. Relevant service-level agreements (SLAs) should detail how quickly the vendor applies critical patches, reports breaches, and restores services after an incident.

CORE QUESTIONS FOR VENDOR ASSESSMENT

• Does the vendor maintain recognized certifications (e.g., ISO 27001, SOC 2)?

• How do they store, encrypt, and back up sensitive data?

• What is their breach notification policy?

ONGOING MONITORING

Risk is never static. Implement a schedule for re-assessments, especially for Tier 1 vendors, which might be reviewed quarterly or semi-annually. If a vendor experiences a breach, immediately evaluate any impact on your organization. Maintaining open communication ensures you receive timely notifications about security updates or incidents. Automated tools can also alert you when a vendor's certification expires or if they appear in breach reports.

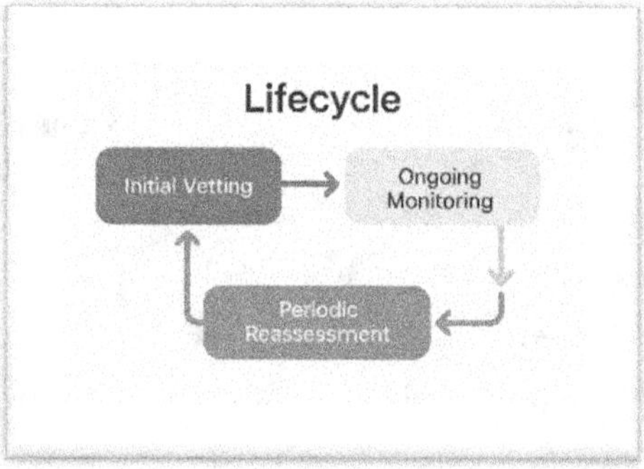

CONTINUOUS OVERSIGHT TIPS

- Monitor vendor security news and advisories
- Request updated audit findings or certifications at least annually
- Maintain contact with vendor representatives for incident disclosures

COMMON PITFALLS

Failing to adjust oversight based on risk level often leads to wasted effort on low-risk suppliers or insufficient scrutiny for critical ones. Generic contracts lacking explicit security obligations can leave you exposed if the vendor's safeguards fall short. Another recurring mistake is assuming a reputable brand equals strong security—well-known companies can still experience breaches. Finally, neglecting to reassess vendors after significant operational changes may leave new vulnerabilities undetected.

AVOIDING ERRORS

• Avoid "one-size-fits-all" reviews; customize based on vendor tier
• Include clear security clauses and breach notification timelines in contracts
• Reevaluate vendors after mergers, product expansions, or staff changes

CONCLUSION

Vendor and SaaS partnerships can be transformative but also expand your attack surface. A structured risk review helps you weigh the benefits of outsourcing against potential security threats.

By categorizing vendors, verifying their practices, and continually monitoring their status, you maintain tighter control over who handles your data and how. This proactive approach not only meets regulatory expectations but also fosters lasting trust with clients and stakeholders who rely on your diligence.

NEXT STEPS

Once you've addressed third-party risks, it's time to examine your overall security posture in a more holistic manner. In Chapter 10: Cybersecurity Assessment or Audit, we'll look at how to conduct a comprehensive evaluation of your defenses. Linking these external vendor reviews with an internal audit process ensures every segment of your organization is protected, integrated, and prepared for whatever cyber threats arise.

CHAPTER 10: CYBERSECURITY ASSESSMENT OR AUDIT

INTRODUCTION

Even the most carefully constructed security program needs validation. A cybersecurity assessment or audit provides an objective snapshot of where your defenses stand—highlighting both strengths and weaknesses. By systematically examining policies, technologies, and user behavior, you can uncover hidden vulnerabilities before attackers do. More than just a "check the box" exercise, a well-executed assessment is a roadmap to continuous improvement, ensuring that you maintain a proactive stance in an ever-changing threat landscape.

WHY AUDITS AND ASSESSMENTS MATTER

Identify Gaps and Risks

Regular assessments uncover overlooked vulnerabilities—such as outdated software, misconfigured firewalls, or weak policies—and prioritize them for remediation.

Validate Security Controls

Even if you have layers of defense in place, an audit tests their effectiveness under realistic conditions (e.g., penetration testing or vulnerability scans).

Regulatory Compliance

Industries with strict standards (e.g., HIPAA, PCI DSS, GDPR) often require documented proof of security audits. Noncompliance can result in hefty fines or legal challenges.

Continuous Improvement

Assessments ensure that your security posture evolves with emerging threats, new technologies, and changes in organizational structure or workflows.

TYPES OF SECURITY ASSESSMENTS

VULNERABILITY SCANS

Automated tools check systems and networks for known security holes, often rating each vulnerability by severity. While a good first step, scans can generate false positives, so manual review is essential.

PENETRATION TESTS (PENTESTS)

Security professionals simulate real-world attacks to see how far they can penetrate your defenses. Pen tests are more in-depth than scans—testers might exploit vulnerabilities, escalate privileges, or attempt lateral movement within the network.

COMPLIANCE OR CERTIFICATION AUDITS

Focuses on meeting specific frameworks or standards (e.g., ISO 27001, SOC 2). An external auditor checks that your policies, procedures, and technical controls align with the required benchmarks.

POLICY & PROCEDURE REVIEWS

Examines whether internal documentation (e.g., incident response plans, HR onboarding/offboarding) is up to date and consistently followed. Even the best tools won't help if processes and training lag behind.

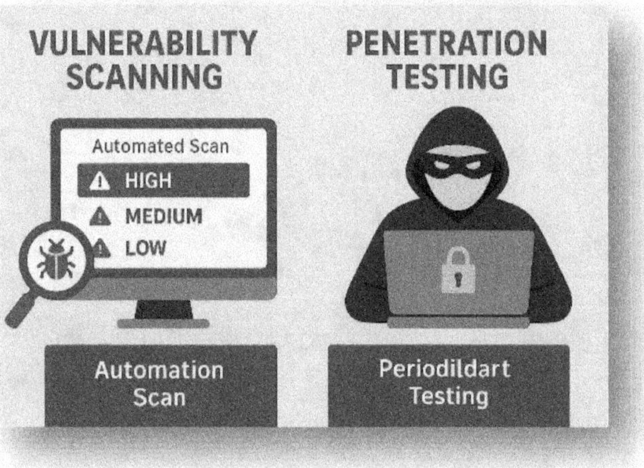

KEY STEPS IN A CYBERSECURITY ASSESSMENT

Define the Scope: Determine which systems, networks, applications, and departments will be audited. A clear, agreed-upon scope prevents misunderstandings later.

Gather Data: Collect relevant documentation (network diagrams, asset inventories, security policies). Run vulnerability scans or interview key personnel if needed.

Evaluate Findings: Compile results, prioritize vulnerabilities, and match each finding to potential impacts on confidentiality, integrity, and availability.

Remediate & Mitigate: Develop action plans for each finding, assigning owners, deadlines, and resources. Quick wins (low effort, high impact) often take priority.

Validate & Report: Re-test after fixes are applied to ensure gaps are truly closed. Document results in a final report that management can use for strategic planning or compliance needs.

ENGAGING EXTERNAL AUDITORS OR CONSULTANTS

Objectivity: A fresh set of eyes may spot issues overlooked by internal teams too familiar with daily operations.

Expertise: External specialists often have hands-on experience with the latest threats, methods, and regulatory developments.

Impartial Assessments: Stakeholders and regulators generally trust external audits more, given the reduced risk of internal bias.

BEST PRACTICES

Establish a Regular Cadence: Schedule full or partial audits annually or biannually. Supplement with targeted checks (e.g., quarterly vulnerability scans) for high-risk systems.

Align with Recognized Frameworks: Use guidelines like NIST CSF, CIS Controls, or ISO 27001 to structure your audit. This ensures comprehensive coverage of technical and procedural areas.

Maintain an Asset Inventory: You can't audit what you don't know exists. Keep an updated list of hardware, software, and cloud services to avoid blind spots.

Focus on Reporting: A well-structured, plain-English report is crucial for leadership to make informed decisions. Highlight critical risks, recommended actions, and potential business impacts.

COMMON PITFALLS

Scope Creep: Without clear boundaries, an audit can balloon in time and cost, or critical systems might get overlooked.

Overreliance on Automated Tools: Tools detect many vulnerabilities, but humans must validate findings. Ignoring manual review leads to false positives or missed threats.

Failure to Follow Up: Conducting an audit without remediating issues defeats the purpose. Lack of remediation plans or accountability leads to repeated vulnerabilities.

Infrequent Assessments: Annual or one-off audits can leave long windows of exposure. Cyber threats evolve quickly, so consistent testing is key.

CONCLUSION

A thorough cybersecurity assessment or audit is one of the best ways to ensure your defenses stay effective over time. By identifying gaps, verifying controls, and regularly testing systems under realistic conditions, organizations remain a step ahead of attackers. When integrated into an ongoing security strategy—alongside patch management, firewalls, user training, and incident response—audits help maintain a robust, flexible posture. They also demonstrate to customers, partners, and regulators that you take your security responsibilities seriously.

NEXT STEPS

With an audit framework in place, you'll have a clearer picture of your strengths and potential blind spots. The next chapter—Chapter 11: Email Filtering/Anti-Phishing—dives into defending one of the most common entry points for malware and social engineering. Building on what you learn from the assessment, you can tailor your email security measures to address the specific risks and weaknesses identified in your audit.

CHAPTER 11: EMAIL FILTERING/ANTI-PHISHING

INTRODUCTION

Email remains one of the most common vectors for cyberattacks. Phishing schemes, malware attachments, and fraudulent links can slip through if effective filtering systems and user education are absent. Even a single successful phishing email can compromise credentials, introduce ransomware, or lead to large-scale data breaches. By deploying robust email filtering solutions and cultivating strong anti-phishing awareness, you significantly reduce the likelihood of costly incidents.

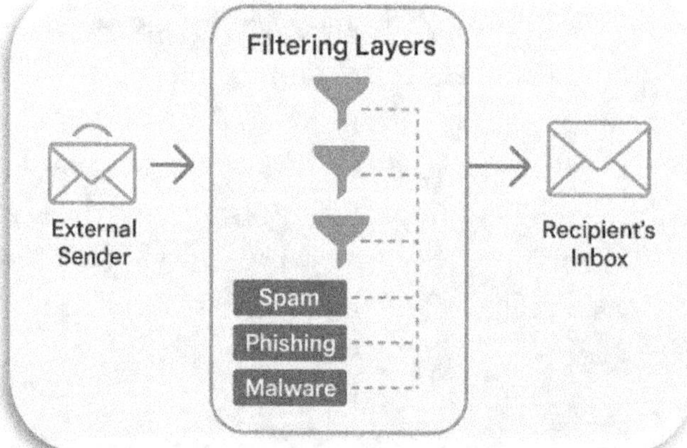

WHY EMAIL FILTERING MATTERS

• **High Volume of Threats**: Attackers exploit email's ubiquity to deliver malicious content at scale.

• **Human Error**: Even tech-savvy users can be fooled by convincing phishing emails, especially under time pressure.

• **Regulatory Concerns**: Many breaches traced back to phishing events violate compliance rules like HIPAA, GDPR, or PCI DSS, leading to fines and reputational harm.

Implementing an advanced filtering system helps you intercept known malicious addresses, suspicious attachments, and spam before they ever reach users' inboxes. Additionally, automated detection technologies leverage machine learning to identify new or evolving threats. When paired with effective user training, email filtering becomes a powerful shield, stopping most attacks before they can even begin.

TYPES OF EMAIL FILTERS

• **Spam Filters**: Block unsolicited or bulk messages, often using reputation-based scores or content analysis.

• **Malware Filters**: Scan attachments and links in real time, quarantining anything deemed dangerous.

• **Phishing Filters**: Look for indicators of deceitful practices—like spoofed addresses, suspicious URLs, or language patterns typical of phishing campaigns.

These filters can exist on-premises via hardware appliances or be integrated into cloud-based email services. Whichever route you choose, ensure the system is routinely updated to reflect the latest threat intelligence. A stagnant filter quickly becomes obsolete as attackers adapt.

CONFIGURING EMAIL FILTERING TOOLS

Fine-tuning filter settings helps maintain a balance between blocking harmful messages and preventing false positives. Overly aggressive filters can flag legitimate emails, causing workflow disruptions. Conversely, lenient rules may allow risky messages to slip through. Set up or integrate with:

• **Blacklists/Blocklists**: Deny emails from known malicious domains or IP addresses.
• **Whitelists/Safelists**: Ensure trusted senders bypass the strictest filtering measures.
• **Quarantine & Review**: Route suspicious messages to a quarantine folder, enabling manual checks before final delivery.

Regularly review filter logs to see which messages were blocked, which were flagged, and which might have been mistakenly quarantined. This process refines accuracy over time, improving the balance between security and productivity.

ANTI-PHISHING BEST PRACTICES

1. **Enable DMARC, DKIM, and SPF**: These email authentication protocols verify the legitimacy of senders, reducing spoofing attempts.
2. **Implement Multi-Factor Authentication**: Even if credentials are stolen via phishing, attackers can't access accounts without the second verification step.
3. **Provide Continuous Training**: Employees should recognize common red flags—such as urgent requests, misspellings, or mismatched URLs.
4. **Encourage Reporting**: Make it easy for users to report suspected phishing attempts, helping security teams act swiftly.

BEHAVIORAL DETECTION & AI

Modern anti-phishing tools use behavioral analysis and machine learning to spot signs that a message may be malicious—even if it hasn't been seen before. These systems examine everything from the sender's email domain and IP reputation to how closely a link's text matches its actual destination. Machine learning models learn from large datasets of spam, phishing, and legitimate emails, refining their detection algorithms over time.

This approach helps catch zero-day phishing attempts, where attackers craft brand-new campaigns not yet cataloged in threat databases. Continuous updates and retraining of models are essential, as cybercriminals consistently innovate to bypass older detection methods.

COMMON PITFALLS

• **Relying Solely on Technology**: Even the best filters miss some attacks. Human awareness and caution remain vital.
• **Ignoring Regular Updates**: Failing to patch or update filtering software leaves vulnerabilities for attackers to exploit.
• **Lax Permissions**: If quarantined items can be released without proper checks, the filtering system's benefits are undone.
• **Overlooking Periodic Reviews**: Not analyzing email logs or user reports means missed opportunities to adapt filtering rules to new threats.

CONCLUSION

Email filtering and anti-phishing measures provide a crucial defensive layer. By combining robust technical tools with strong user awareness, you prevent most malicious emails from ever landing in an inbox, and you empower recipients to deal safely with suspicious messages that do slip through.

This two-pronged strategy not only protects sensitive data but also nurtures a culture of vigilance throughout your organization. As you refine configurations and train your team, your defenses become increasingly difficult for attackers to penetrate—ensuring that email remains a productive communication channel rather than a security liability.

NEXT STEPS

Equipping employees to identify and manage email-based threats is vital, but so is securing the devices they use to access those messages. In Chapter 12: Mobile Device Management (MDM), we'll explore strategies for safeguarding smartphones, tablets, and other mobile endpoints—tools that have become essential to modern workflows but also present unique security challenges.

CHAPTER 12: MOBILE DEVICE MANAGEMENT (MDM)

INTRODUCTION

Smartphones, tablets, and other mobile endpoints have become indispensable in modern business. They enable flexible work arrangements, instant communication, and on-the-go productivity. However, the same mobility that powers efficiency also introduces significant risks: unsecured Wi-Fi connections, lost or stolen devices, and the potential for mixing personal and corporate data. A robust Mobile Device Management (MDM) strategy helps address these challenges by enforcing security policies, monitoring device activity, and streamlining updates. Organizations that neglect MDM often find themselves vulnerable to data breaches, compliance violations, and reputational damage.

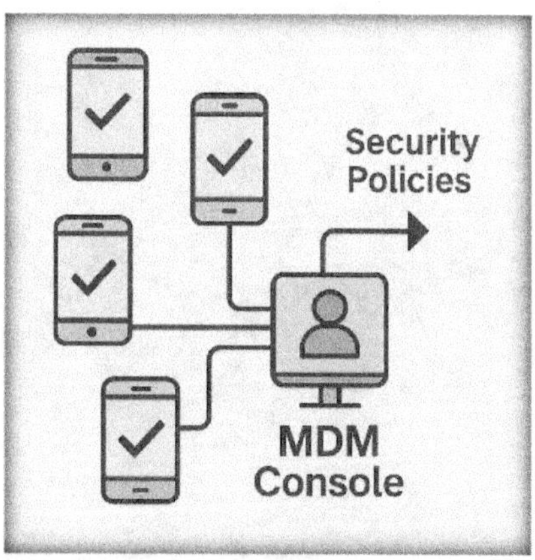

WHY MDM MATTERS

- **Variety of Devices**: Employees use a range of personal and corporate-owned phones and tablets, each with its own operating system, version, and update schedule.
- **Data Protection**: Mobile devices can store sensitive information—customer records, confidential emails, corporate documents—that must remain secure at all times.
- **Regulatory Pressures**: Industries like healthcare, finance, and e-commerce face stringent data handling requirements. Unsecured mobile endpoints can lead to serious compliance breaches.

MDM solutions enable IT administrators to deploy consistent security settings across diverse devices. Encryption enforcement, password requirements, and app installation rules help maintain a stable baseline of protection. If a device is lost or stolen, MDM software can remotely lock or wipe data, minimizing the damage from unauthorized access.

KEY FEATURES OF MDM

- **Centralized Management**: A single console to track, monitor, and configure devices, simplifying complex environments.

- **Application Control**: Restrict or whitelist certain apps to prevent unauthorized software from running on corporate devices.
- **Secure Content Distribution**: Provide encrypted documents and files safely to mobile endpoints, reducing reliance on insecure channels.

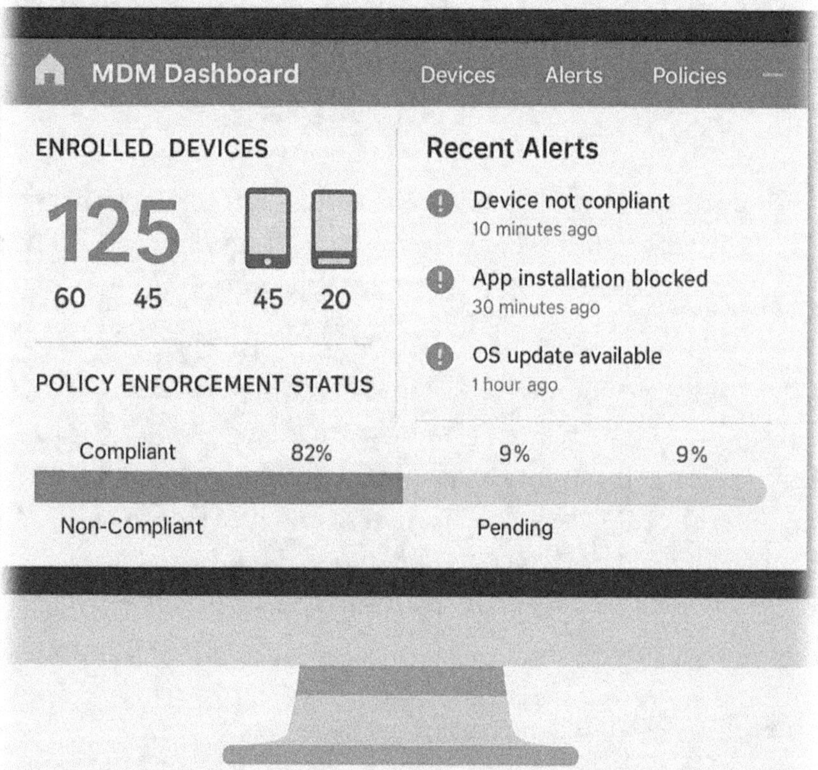

CONFIGURING MDM STRATEGIES

An effective MDM plan often involves separating personal and corporate data on the same device, commonly referred to as containerization. This isolation ensures that personal apps and files can't tap into business information. Similarly, MDM policies might dictate how often devices must check in with the central console for updates, or whether certain geolocation services are enabled.

When rolling out MDM, consider user experience. Strict policies that inhibit normal device use can result in pushback, prompting employees to circumvent security controls. Conversely, overly lax policies put critical data at risk. Finding a balance—where security is robust but not onerous—often involves pilot programs, user feedback, and iterative adjustments.

BEST PRACTICES

REGULAR UPDATES & PATCHES

Mobile operating systems frequently release security patches addressing newly discovered vulnerabilities. MDM platforms can automate these updates, ensuring that all devices remain current without relying on end-users to act promptly.

ENFORCE AUTHENTICATION STANDARDS

Require strong passcodes or biometric locks to prevent unauthorized access. Combine this with remote wipe capabilities, so if a device is compromised, sensitive data can be erased immediately.

CLEAR ACCEPTABLE USE POLICIES

Define which apps and websites employees can access on corporate devices. Spell out the consequences for jailbreaking or rooting a phone, along with guidance on safe personal use if you permit it on business devices.

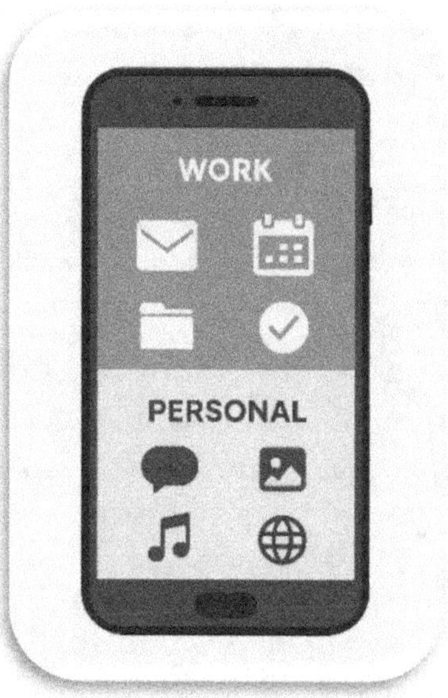

COMMON PITFALLS

- **Inconsistent Rollout**: Allowing some departments or regions to opt out of MDM weakens overall security, leaving gaps that attackers can exploit.
- **Neglecting User Education**: Employees unaware of MDM policies may violate them accidentally, storing data in insecure apps or bypassing device checks.

- **One-Size-Fits-All Policies**: Different roles or teams may require unique settings. Overly uniform restrictions can impede legitimate business tasks.
- **Poor Monitoring**: Failing to review alerts or usage reports means you might miss warning signs of compromised devices or rogue apps.

CONCLUSION

Mobile Device Management serves as a vital component of any modern cybersecurity strategy. By implementing device-level controls, enforcing consistent security measures, and maintaining visibility over app usage, organizations can empower their workforce to stay productive on the go—without sacrificing protection. Balancing user experience with robust safeguards takes thoughtful planning, pilot testing, and ongoing refinements. The result is a more resilient, agile environment in which mobile endpoints complement rather than compromise your overall security posture.

NEXT STEPS

With mobile devices under control, the next logical step is to ensure that all data—whether on a phone, server, or in transit—remains protected against unauthorized access. In Chapter 13: Data Encryption (at rest + transit), we'll delve into how encryption fortifies sensitive information, both when stored and while moving across networks. This final layer of protection further strengthens your defenses against eavesdroppers and data thieves.

CHAPTER 13: DATA ENCRYPTION (AT REST + TRANSIT)

INTRODUCTION

Data encryption is fundamental to safeguarding sensitive information against unauthorized access and interception. Whether storing financial records on a server or sending confidential messages across the internet, robust encryption scrambles data so it's unreadable without the correct decryption key. In an era where breaches and eavesdropping attempts abound, encryption acts as an essential shield—protecting both the integrity and privacy of your data. By implementing encryption at rest and in transit, organizations create multiple barriers that deter attackers from viewing or manipulating sensitive assets.

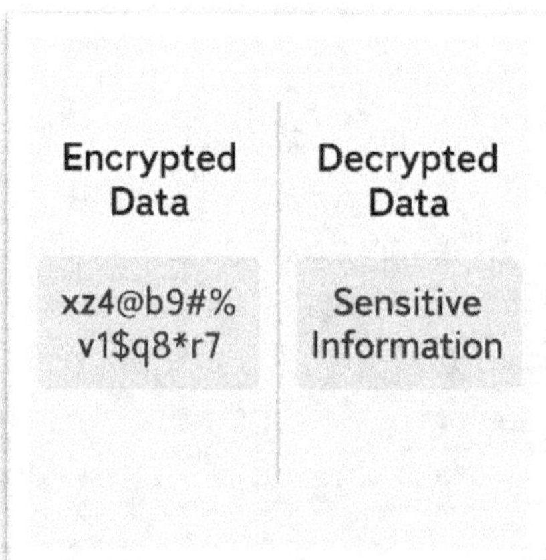

WHY ENCRYPTION MATTERS

- **Regulatory Compliance**: Many laws and standards (HIPAA, GDPR, PCI DSS) mandate encryption for sensitive data, requiring businesses to prove its usage in case of audits or breaches.
- **Trust and Reputation**: Customers and partners expect strong safeguards around any personal or financial details they share. Encryption demonstrates proactive diligence.
- **Defense in Depth**: Even if attackers bypass perimeter security or intercept data mid-transit, properly encrypted information remains virtually unintelligible.

Encryption isn't just a checkbox item. It's a core practice that complements firewalls, access control, and other security measures. Failing to deploy encryption means leaving a major gap in your defenses, especially if employees store valuable data on removable drives, cloud platforms, or mobile devices.

ENCRYPTION AT REST

Encryption at rest protects stored data—from databases and file servers to portable drives and smartphones. The process ensures that, without the right key, the data appears as meaningless code. Common methods include:

- Full Disk Encryption: Protects everything on a device's hard drive, locking down data if the hardware is stolen or lost.

- File/Folder Encryption: Allows selective encryption of specific directories, especially useful for shared servers where not all data needs the same level of protection.
- Database Encryption: Safeguards stored records at the application level, making them indecipherable if unauthorized individuals gain direct access.

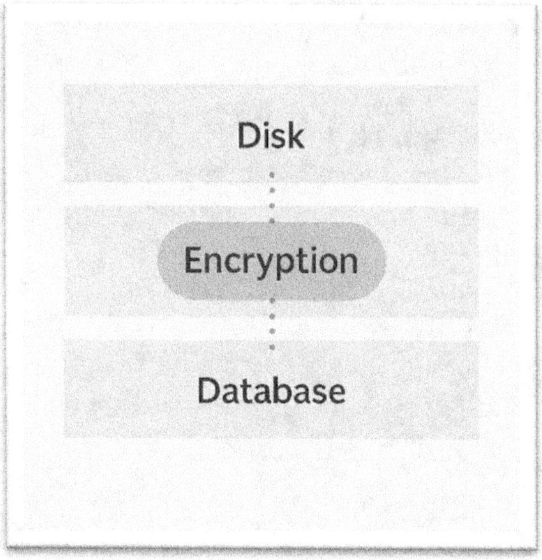

An essential consideration is key management. If encryption keys are stored insecurely on the same system they protect, adversaries may simply retrieve those keys. Secure key storage mechanisms—such as Hardware Security Modules (HSMs) or dedicated key management services—reduce that risk significantly.

ENCRYPTION IN TRANSIT

Whenever data is sent across networks—from email attachments to remote server requests—encryption in transit protects against interception. Protocols like HTTPS (for web traffic) and TLS (for email or other data streams) encrypt information before it leaves the sender's endpoint, ensuring it remains safe until the intended recipient decrypts it.

Best practices include:

- **Using TLS/SSL for Website Connections**: Ensuring all pages (not just login screens) use HTTPS helps maintain a secure channel, preventing attackers from snooping or altering traffic.
- **Email Encryption**: Transport Layer Security (TLS) and solutions like PGP or S/MIME protect message contents against unauthorized viewing.
- **VPN Tunnels**: Establishing an encrypted tunnel for remote access keeps sensitive data hidden, even on untrusted networks.

COMMON PITFALLS

1. **Weak or Outdated Algorithms**: Relying on legacy ciphers (e.g., MD5, SHA-1, or older SSL versions) can lead to easy decryption by modern methods. Regularly update to strong algorithms like AES and current TLS standards.
2. **Improper Key Management**: Storing encryption keys with the encrypted data, reusing keys across multiple systems, or failing to rotate keys can compromise the entire encryption scheme.
3. **Performance Concerns**: While encryption can introduce overhead, failing to optimize or balance encryption settings sometimes leads teams to disable or skip it. Proper planning and modern hardware minimize performance hits.
4. **Overlooking Human Factors**: Encryption policies won't help if employees store keys in plaintext files, use weak passwords, or transmit unencrypted files via email. Ongoing training and clear guidelines are essential.

CONCLUSION

Effective encryption strategies safeguard data both at rest and in transit, forming a crucial part of any layered cybersecurity approach. By choosing the right encryption methods, managing keys securely, and keeping abreast of evolving cryptographic standards, you ensure that sensitive information remains inaccessible to unauthorized parties. Whether a server is compromised or network traffic is intercepted, properly encrypted data often remains indecipherable, saving organizations from the worst outcomes of a breach.

As technology evolves, encryption will remain central to protecting privacy and maintaining trust with customers, partners, and regulators alike. Coupled with vigilant employee training and consistent policy enforcement, strong encryption practices make breaching your environment considerably more difficult for even the most determined adversaries.

NEXT STEPS

Encrypting data is crucial, but ensuring secure remote connections is equally important. In Chapter 14: VPN for Remote Work, we'll explore how Virtual Private Networks provide encrypted tunnels for offsite access, protecting corporate networks and sensitive data from prying eyes—no matter where employees are working.

CHAPTER 14: VPN FOR REMOTE WORK

INTRODUCTION

As remote and hybrid work models become the norm, ensuring secure access to internal systems is more important than ever. Whether working from home, a coffee shop, or an airport lounge, employees often connect to corporate networks using public or untrusted Wi-Fi.

These environments expose data transmissions to risks like interception, session hijacking, and man-in-the-middle attacks. A Virtual Private Network (VPN) acts as a secure, encrypted tunnel between users and your organization's network, shielding data from prying eyes and reducing the risk of unauthorized access.

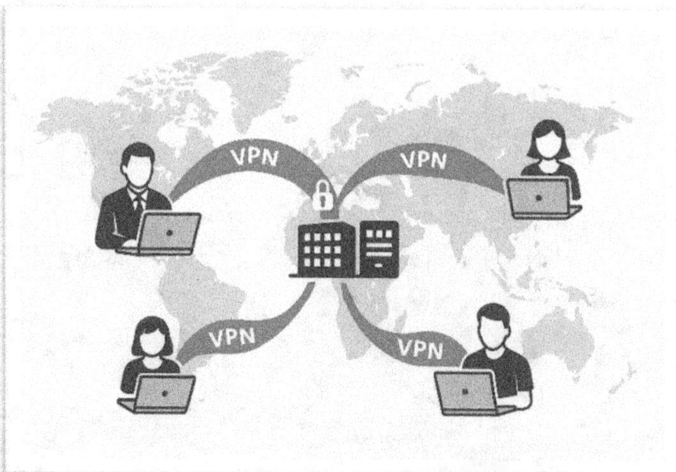

WHY VPNs ARE ESSENTIAL FOR SECURITY

- **Data Privacy on Public Networks**: Without a VPN, data transmitted over open Wi-Fi can be intercepted by attackers monitoring the same network.
- **Access Control**: VPNs enable businesses to enforce secure authentication before granting access to internal tools and systems.
- **Location Masking**: VPNs can route traffic through secure endpoints, masking IP addresses and reducing the risk of targeted attacks based on location data.

By encrypting all traffic between a remote device and the corporate network, a VPN protects emails, files, and credentials—even when sent across insecure networks.

TYPES OF VPN SOLUTIONS

REMOTE ACCESS VPN

Commonly used by employees working from outside the office. It creates a secure, encrypted connection from the user's device to the internal company network.

SITE-TO-SITE VPN

Connects two networks (e.g., branch offices) securely over the internet. It's ideal for organizations with multiple locations that need to share resources privately.

CLOUD VPN / ZERO TRUST NETWORK ACCESS (ZTNA)

Modern cloud-based VPN alternatives offer better scalability and integrate Zero Trust principles—granting access based on user identity and device trustworthiness rather than physical location.

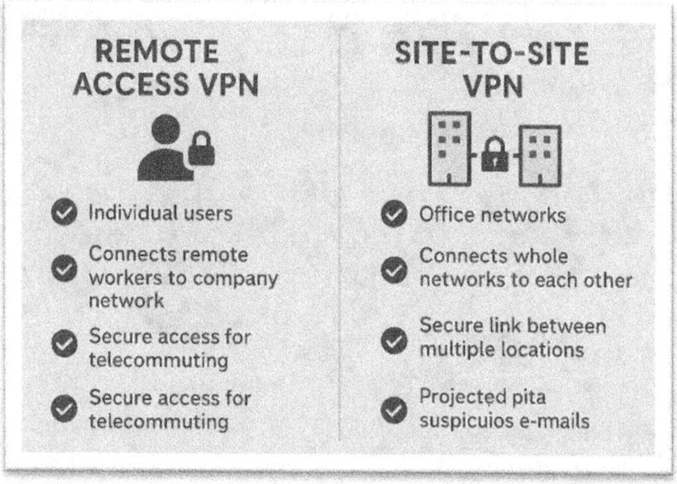

BEST PRACTICES FOR VPN DEPLOYMENT

1. **Use Strong Encryption Protocols**
   Ensure your VPN uses secure encryption standards such as OpenVPN, WireGuard, or IPsec. Avoid legacy protocols like PPTP, which have known vulnerabilities.

2. **Enforce Multi-Factor Authentication (MFA)**
   Adding a second layer of authentication ensures that even if VPN credentials are stolen, unauthorized access is still blocked.
3. **Split Tunneling Control**
   Decide whether to allow users to access public internet content outside the VPN tunnel. Disabling split tunneling routes all traffic through the VPN, offering maximum protection—but may impact performance.
4. **Monitor and Log Activity**
   Track VPN usage to detect anomalies, such as logins from unusual geographic locations, excessive file downloads, or off-hours access.

COMMON PITFALLS

- **Neglecting Updates**: Using outdated VPN clients or servers can leave organizations exposed to known vulnerabilities.
- **Poor User Experience**: A VPN that slows down internet access may lead employees to disable it, undermining security.
- **Over-Permissive Access**: Giving all users full network access increases the attack surface. Apply the principle of least privilege by limiting what each user can access via the VPN.
- **Weak Authentication**: VPNs relying only on usernames and passwords are highly vulnerable to phishing or credential-stuffing attacks.

COMBINING VPN WITH ZERO TRUST

VPNs offer excellent protection for traditional perimeter-based architectures, but they are not a complete solution on their own—especially in cloud-first environments. Integrating Zero Trust Network Access (ZTNA) principles with VPN setups helps shift focus from "network access" to "resource-level access," ensuring users are only allowed to interact with systems they are explicitly authorized to use. This hybrid model enhances both usability and control.

CONCLUSION

VPNs remain a foundational tool in the modern cybersecurity stack, especially for organizations with remote or mobile workforces. When properly configured and supported by strong authentication, monitoring, and user education, VPNs offer a secure and private channel for accessing internal systems from anywhere in the world. They prevent sensitive data from falling into the wrong hands and help ensure regulatory compliance even when employees are scattered across time zones and countries.

As work continues to evolve beyond the traditional office, securing the connections that link people to company infrastructure will remain a priority. VPNs, especially when combined with Zero Trust principles, help strike the right balance between access and security—allowing businesses to stay agile without compromising protection.

NEXT STEPS

Protecting infrastructure is crucial—but what if things still go wrong? That's where financial resilience comes into play. In Chapter 15: Cyber Insurance, we'll explore how cybersecurity insurance policies can help organizations recover from the aftermath of a breach or attack. From ransomware payouts to legal defense, we'll break down how cyber insurance fits into your broader risk management strategy.

CHAPTER 15: CYBER INSURANCE

INTRODUCTION

Cyber insurance has quickly become an essential safeguard for organizations of all sizes. Even with strong security controls, breaches and attacks can still occur. Cyber insurance helps mitigate the financial fallout, covering costs from legal defense and breach notifications to ransom payments and system recovery. By providing a financial backstop, cyber insurance plays a pivotal role in an organization's broader risk management strategy.

WHY CYBER INSURANCE MATTERS

Data Breach Expenses: Policies can help cover forensic investigations, legal fees, regulatory fines, and breach notification costs.

Ransomware and Extortion: Some insurers will reimburse or directly cover ransom payments—though this can be a complex area due to evolving regulations and ethical considerations.

Business Interruption: If critical systems are taken offline by an attack, insurance can offset the revenue lost during downtime.

Third-Party Liability: Organizations may face lawsuits or claims from customers or partners whose data was compromised in a breach. Cyber insurance can cover defense costs and settlements.

Without cyber insurance, even a single significant incident can strain or cripple an organization's finances. By offsetting these risks, organizations can recover faster, maintain stakeholder trust, and continue operating with minimal disruption.

KEY TYPES OF COVERAGE

DATA BREACH RESPONSE

Covers costs for forensic analysis, notification of affected parties, credit monitoring services, and legal consultations.

RANSOMWARE & EXTORTION

May include the cost of ransom payments and related expenses, though coverage specifics can vary greatly based on insurer policies and legal restrictions.

BUSINESS INTERRUPTION

Reimburses lost revenue, ongoing operational costs, and sometimes additional expenditures related to the incident's downtime.

THIRD-PARTY CLAIMS

Protects against lawsuits brought by clients, vendors, or partners claiming damages from a security breach originating in your environment.

BEST PRACTICES FOR SELECTING A POLICY

- **Policy Limits**: Evaluate worst-case scenarios and choose coverage limits that adequately address those risks.
- **Exclusions and Exceptions**: Understand exactly what is and isn't covered, such as "acts of war" or state-sponsored attacks.
- **Retroactive Coverage**: Some breaches go unnoticed for months. Look for policies that offer coverage for incidents discovered after the policy start date but initiated beforehand.
- **Panel of Providers**: Many insurers require (or strongly recommend) using specific legal, forensic, and PR firms. Verify their quality and ensure they align with your organization's needs.
- **Cost-Benefit Analysis**: Compare premium costs with the potential financial impact of a large-scale incident. Premiums may be high, but a single, uninsured breach could be far more expensive in both direct costs and reputational damage.

FILING A CLAIM & WORKING WITH INSURERS

1. **Follow Your Incident Response Plan:** Stop the bleeding first—contain the attack, preserve evidence, and engage your response team.

2. **Notify Your Insurer Promptly:** Delays could result in denied or reduced claims. Insurers may require specific vendors or processes for incident management.
3. **Document Everything:** Maintain detailed records of timelines, costs, decisions, and communications. Insurers rely on this documentation to validate claims.
4. **Collaborate with the Adjuster:** The insurer's claims adjuster will likely conduct an investigation. Provide them with the necessary data while ensuring they do not disrupt remediation efforts.

COMMON PITFALLS

- **Unclear Exclusions**: Some policies have narrow definitions of covered events, leading to claim denials when incidents fall into grey areas.
- **Insufficient Coverage Limits**: Underestimating the scale of potential breaches can leave significant expenses uncovered.
- **Failure to Maintain Security Controls**: If policy terms mandate certain controls—like encryption or multi-factor authentication—failing to keep them up to date can void coverage.
- **Assuming Insurance Replaces Security**: Cyber insurance is a complement to, not a substitute for, strong cybersecurity practices. An insurer may raise premiums or deny coverage if fundamental security measures are lacking.

COMBINING CYBER INSURANCE WITH RISK MANAGEMENT

Cyber insurance works best when it's part of a comprehensive approach to security:

- **Preventive Measures**: Insurers increasingly require evidence of robust controls. The better your security posture, the more favorable your premiums and coverage terms can be.
- **Incident Response Planning**: Well-documented response strategies help minimize damages and streamline the claims process.
- **Continuous Improvement**: Monitor emerging threats, adjust policies, and ensure compliance with insurer requirements to keep coverage valid and effective.

CONCLUSION

Cyber insurance offers organizations a critical safety net in today's threat landscape. While no policy can prevent attacks, having the right coverage can mean the difference between a swift recovery and an existential crisis. When integrated with strong cybersecurity controls and a proactive incident response plan, cyber insurance empowers organizations to face evolving threats with greater resilience and confidence.

This chapter concludes our journey through the foundational elements of a modern cybersecurity program. From securing remote connections to ensuring financial resilience, each piece contributes to a layered defense strategy. As the threat landscape continually evolves, stay proactive: regularly review and update both technical defenses and insurance policies. By combining robust preventive measures with a solid financial backup plan, your organization will be well-prepared for whatever challenges come next.

Thank You

Thank you for taking the time to read this eBook. We hope the information provided has been insightful and will help you strengthen your cybersecurity defenses. If you need additional support, guidance, or services, we at AcraSolution are here to help. Alongside our paid offerings, we also maintain a growing library of **free resources**, including documentation, articles, and practical guides that can bring you immediate value—no strings attached. Feel free to visit our website or reach out directly—together, we can build a more secure future.

— ***Eric LeBouthillier***
Author & Cybersecurity Strategist

www.ingramcontent.com/pod-product-compliance
Lightning Source LLC
LaVergne TN
LVHW022311200926
848481LV00004B/1280
* 9 7 8 1 0 6 9 6 4 3 7 7 3 *